TINY H

Effective Tips and Techniques for Designing, Building

(Everything You Should Know Before Buying a Tiny House)

Alfred Ojeda

Published by Tomas Edwards

© **Alfred Ojeda**

All Rights Reserved

Tiny House: Effective Tips and Techniques for Designing, Building (Everything You Should Know Before Buying a Tiny House)

ISBN 978-1-990268-99-1

Legal & Disclaimer

The information contained in this book is not designed to replace or take the place of any form of medicine or professional medical advice. The information in this book has been provided for educational and entertainment purposes only.

The information contained in this book has been compiled from sources deemed reliable, and it is accurate to the best of the Author's knowledge; however, the Author cannot guarantee its accuracy and validity and cannot be held liable for any errors or omissions. Changes are periodically made to this book. You must consult your doctor or get professional medical advice before using any of the suggested remedies, techniques, or information in this book.

Upon using the information contained in this book, you agree to hold harmless the Author from and against any damages, costs, and expenses, including any legal fees potentially resulting from the application of any of the information provided by this guide. This disclaimer applies to any damages or injury caused by the use and application, whether directly or indirectly, of any advice or information presented, whether for breach of contract, tort, negligence, personal injury, criminal intent, or under any other cause of action.

You agree to accept all risks of using the information presented inside this book. You need to consult a professional medical practitioner in order to ensure you are both able and healthy enough to participate in this program.

Table of Contents

Introduction

There are so many people who often dream of living in huge houses for quite a number few reasons. Some are because they wish to show off to their friends while others want to live to a great houses that are luxurious to feel comfortable and fit in a given social class.

However, there are some of us that do not wish to spend a lot of money paying mortgages and utility bills that come along with an enormous house. If you are just like me, then this is the book for you! Tiny houses are cost-effective houses that you can build and live simply.

This book serves as a guide for beginners who wish to build their tiny house based on their budget. You will learn the various factors that you have to consider before building a tiny house and simple steps that will bring you from having no house to owning a tiny house. Yes, I mean owning your tiny house!

This means that if you are determined to create your space that is customized to fit your taste, then this is the right book for you. With a tiny house, you can do many things yourself. This means that you save up on labor costs as well as design the house to suit your taste and personality.

Additionally, if you are not confident in yourself to create designs for your tiny house, you can have an expert do this for you at a lower price. This is a great book in creating a tiny house that can be contemporary, eclectic, Scandinavian, traditional or coastal in nature.

This often gives you the freedom to create a space that is unique to you and is comfortable and meets all your need. With a tiny house, you will learn to appreciate the benefits that come along with minimalist lifestyles.

You will eventually realize how much you have been missing and thus, will not wish to the kind of living arrangement you had. Because of your tiny house, you life's perspective and style will be changed for the better!

You have to realize that creating tiny house plans is not meant for those that are weak at heart. This means that it does not discriminate on personality, social class, age, rate among other factors.

Creating your tiny house only requires your commitment and readiness to owning your space. This is because one of the greatest challenges is creating your home by building it right from scratch. You have to be ready in all aspects. The building project often starts out innocently and before long, it escalates into a hectic job that if you are not robust and resilient enough, you might end up frustrated.

But what you have to bear in mind for a fact is that the results of the house are gratifying enough. This is similar to cultivating a vegetable garden from dirt to a beautiful garden full of great food to feed the family!

Chapter 1: The Tiny House Regime

What is tiny living? Do you understand what is meant by tiny house movement?

In simple words, it's the social movement whereby most people are downsizing their living space and embracing tiny houses. A typical home in America is approximately 2, 600 square feet and typical tiny or small houses range from 100-400 square feet. You can find tiny houses in all forms, shapes and sizes and they offer simpler living in spaces which are smaller but more efficient.

People have different reasons as to why they have or are joining the movement, but the most popular and common reasons include financial concerns, desire for more freedom and time and environmental concerns. For most people, ½ or 1/3 of their monthly or weekly income is directed towards rentals; over your lifetime, this translates to approximately 15 working years. Therefore, living smaller proves to be the only solution.

Why Have Tiny Houses?

Imagine a life free from utility bills, mortgage and rent; living without having to worry about capturing water or generating electricity. Well, the truth is, you can build such a home at a pocket-friendly price. Living free from debt would positively change or make your life different; a bigger life.

Tiny homes are concerned with living simply, with the things you need and yet, beautifully. The environmental benefits of 'living small' are of more paramount significance than the economic and financial advantages. Tiny homes are coupled with smaller environmental footprint, which, in general, encourages less consumption since consumption of resources by humans is mitigated; they advocate for more simplistic living lifestyles, and the possibility for a future which is more sustainable, is opened up.

Traditionally, the tiny houses are approximately 2.4 x 5 meters, containing a bathroom, living area, kitchen and a sleeping loft. The house is constructed in a way that it fits a trailer, so as to make it easy to move. This revolutionises home ownership or takes home ownership to a new level since you're able to own a house, without necessarily having to purchase or own the land that you've parked your tiny house on. The houses can also be designed as self-contained or off-grid, generating electricity and water.

Cheap Housing Revolution: Tiny House Movement

You may have many unanswered questions concerning the small homes movement. You need to get answers to the questions and this is exactly where the e book comes in.

The 'Tiny House Movement', also referred to as the "Small House Movement", is the growing settlement trend where a majority of the people are shifting their preference from the behemoth homes to smaller homes. But what size is tiny? Well, tiny is subject to opinion and debate since all circumstances are relative. However, most people view tiny as a size ranging from 65 square feet to 400 square feet.

The size of small homes depends on the inhabitants' lifestyles and the number of occupants; most small houses fall in the 400-1700 square feet bracket. In most cases, what most people in the housing world view to be small is a size between 400-1000 square feet; but again, it's a matter of opinion.

Not a lot of importance is associated with the square footage as many presume it to be. The most important thing is for your needs to be met right from your home, nothing more. And yes, it's inclusive of your family members, unless you won't live with them.

The real message that the simple living and housing movement advocates for is being conscious of all aspects of how we live. This not only includes the consumption and purchasing decisions but also the deeper things such as making life goals and getting what we want by getting rid of some 'baggage'.

Facts on Housing

According to a census in 2010, 2,392 square feet was the average size for homes in the U.S. This figure is a reduced square footage dating back in 2007 when 2,521 square feet was the average size. On the same chart, in 1973, 1660 square feet was the average size. These changes clearly prove that the calculation or averaging of these sizes is not constant, but rather subject to opinion.

The truth is, you can significantly reduce the risk of financial ruin in case you're sacked by reducing your rental expenditure. Therefore, it's incredibly brilliant to join the movement and shift to 'living small' in a tiny or small house. Tiny houses have many advantages (as discussed later on in the book). However, smaller homes save you money and time. More importantly, they offer the peace of mind since the thought of you doing what's good for your environmental, satisfies you.

Living Big by Living Small

Yes, as ironic as it sounds, it's the absolute truth. Take a moment and ponder on it. You can live to your maximum by living in a small or tiny home; downsize for a reason. Living small helps you to live big by getting rid of the unused or unwanted stuff. Living small is all about de-cluttering your life.

Living small not only helps you to simplify your home by clearing the clutter or making it smaller but can also:

Simplify your relationships

Simplify your business or job duties

Simplify your routines for exercising

Simplify your meals

Simplify your attitude

Simplify your thoughts

It's these little changes that add up and contribute to a significant positive outcome in your living, either right away or later on.

Chapter 2: Tiny Living And Minimalism

A lot of people are following the trend of tiny living, which benefits them in many ways. While many people think that having a larger space is better and means that you are more successful in life, this is not always the case. The tiny house movement helps people to live simpler lives in smaller spaces. These homes are usually less than 400 square feet but have enough space for most people. People opting for a tiny living are driven by many reasons, one of which is the attempt to move away from a mindset that is consumerism driven.

As you read on, you will learn how to adjust to tiny living in many different ways. This book is a detailed guide to help anyone get accustomed to a tiny home and utilize all the space in it to its maximum potential. That is where minimalism comes in. Getting rid of the excess in your life and home will benefit you in more ways than one. Having fewer things in your home will allow the smallest space to look bigger. It will also help you to optimize the space you have and live a simpler life.

The traditional homes that most of us live in have a lot of square footage. People think that acquiring homes with maximum square footage is a sign of success. They just want all the space to fill their homes with more material possessions that demonstrate success. Such homes feel like storage units or a place to pay homage to certain things. The designs of such houses focus on where items should be placed. In tiny homes, the designs are focused on how people will interact with each other and the best way in which they can live in their homes.

The designs include the use of light, materials, and space in a lot more intentional ways in tiny living, which makes it drastically different from traditional homes. In a tiny house, you escape the trap of consumerism and live a much happier life. When you move towards tiny living, you start asking yourself many important questions. You start to think of what is important in your life and what your needs or wants are. You will realize the role consumerism has played in determining what you want from your life.

With the practice of tiny living and minimalism, you will be able to change the habits that have a negative impact on your life and instead move towards a life of wellbeing.

Tiny living focuses on three main principles.

- The effective use of whatever space is available to you.

- To meet the needs of its residents through great design.

- To act as a tool that allows the residents to live the life they truly want and can be happy in.

Tiny houses are of different sizes, and there is no specific square footage that will determine the house as a tiny one. While some people opt for extremely tiny homes and some tiny homes are larger, here we will focus on those that go up to 400 square feet. The number of people who will live in the house is usually a determining factor of how big or small the house can be.

Regardless of the space, anyone living in a tiny home has to be more intentional about how they use the space in the house. This is why tiny homes are not just about the size of the house but are a lifestyle of "tiny living." People who live in tiny homes are much more conscious about the decisions they make and use the benefits of tiny living to its utmost potential. This allows them to improve their social, mental, financial, and physical wellbeing all at the same time. They realize that living in large homes and aiming to upgrade the size of their homes constantly does not really benefit them in any way.

Instead, it adds stress, anxiety, and problems in their lives. They lead to unsatisfied and unfulfilled lives. Tiny living allows them to change all this. Minimalism is a crucial aspect of tiny living, and with this book, you will be able to adopt the tiny living lifestyle in the simplest way possible.

Tiny Living Benefits

Financial Freedom

One of the most obvious and important benefits is that you save a lot of money. Statistics show that more than half the people who live in tiny homes are completely free from credit card debt. They also don't have mortgage payments that most people with larger homes have to deal with.

Building a tiny home costs a lot less money and instead allows you to save more. You can build a tiny home with every necessary convenience and save more compared to buying a traditional larger home. These homes can be designed to last longer and be more functional at low costs.

The minimalist lifestyle that goes hand in hand with tiny living is another reason that your finances fare better. You have to think twice before you bring possessions into smaller spaces, so you are less likely to make impulsive buys. Your spending habits improve significantly over time. You will also have more money to spend on things you actually want or need because of your savings.

Easier to Move

Most tiny homes are mobile. A tiny home can be built in a way that it can be moved at any time. With a traditional home, you will be tied down to the property. A tiny home can be parked on any plot of land you buy. If you decide to move to a new city, you can easily drive the house to that place and just sell the old plot. You don't have to think twice about grabbing better opportunities in other places.

Environmental Consciousness

Tiny homes take a lot less space and very little resources to build and maintain. This means that you leave a smaller carbon footprint. The house can be built with sustainable and recycled materials. You can also find a lot of salvaged or repurposed materials for construction as well as decor. Tiny homes are also very energy efficient compared to traditional homes. A lot of tiny homeowners tend to opt for sustainable energy sources like solar panels to meet their energy needs. You will have a lot fewer appliances and fewer energy needs, and reduce wastage of energy.

Reduced Anxiety

One of the principal benefits of minimalism and tiny living is mental wellbeing. Living in a big house and having a materialistic lifestyle brings a lot of anxiety. The more you own, the more you have to maintain it. You will spend a lot of money and time on unnecessary things. With this new way of living, you can live a more wholesome life and reduce anxiety on so many levels. You have less to worry about, and your materialistic needs decrease as well, thus reducing stress. A tiny minimalist home will instill a sense of peace within you.

More Space

The less you own, the more space you have in your home. Having too many things will only eat up the little space you have and cause clutter. As you declutter each part of your home, you will see more space on your desk, a more organized wardrobe, a cleaner kitchen, etc. Having all this space freed up will make your home look bigger, cleaner, and a lot more organized.

Charity

Another benefit is that you can help others while you shift to tiny living and minimalism. There are so many belongings that you don't use, but others might need it. When you are getting rid of the clutter, make a pile of things that others could benefit from. You might have some emotional attachment to certain things, but giving them away to the needy will make the process much easier for you. You will find a new home for things that you love instead of throwing them away. Donating to the less fortunate is a way to build on your character and feel happy even while you declutter your own home.

Sense of Control

Everyone aims to have a certain level of control in their lives. However, despite all their efforts, this is not always possible. There is a lot in your life that you may not be able to control, but your home and the way you live should not be one of them. Cultivating the habits of minimalism and living in a tiny home will give you a sense of control that other aspects of your life might not give you. You get to make small but significant decisions about what you buy, keep or give away all the time. This allows you to lead a more disciplined life and have pride in your decisions.

More Time

Time is precious and has to be utilized in the best way possible. If you have a very big house with too many things, you waste a lot of time dealing with it. Unless you want the house to be dirty or messy, you need to set aside time to clean and organize every day. This can be extremely time-consuming when there are too much space and too many possessions. However, with tiny living, you just need a few minutes every day to maintain a beautiful home. You won't see a chair piled up with clothes or dust gathering on things you don't use. Being able to spend less time on all these mundane tasks will allow you to be more productive in other ways and also have more time to relax.

Regardless of what the size the house is or what items you personally need, you will see that tiny living has many advantages and is an undeniably great way to live. Considering all the benefits we have mentioned, it is surprising that more people haven't made the shift to tiny living yet. However, the numbers are on the rise every day, and we are glad that you are one of them. You will lead a happier and less stressful life this way.

Chapter 3:Evolution Of Tiny Houses

So what are tiny houses? Tiny houses as the name implies refers to small houses which are typically smaller than 1000 square feet. Some places also imply that tiny houses are smaller than 400 square feet.

The reason for their evolution was simple as at the time of economic crisis, people thought this to be a viable option. Due to a smaller utilization of land, they are obviously cheaper to buy, build and maintain. In addition, a small space can accommodate lesser stuff and hence it encourages a simpler living. Therefore, it was an efficient means of saving up on finances.

Soon people realized that there were other benefits as well as other uses of these tiny houses which enabled them to grow in popularity. With the right architecture, you can build a stylish, simple little house to live in. People preferring a simple lifestyle also find tiny houses very comforting. Hence, finances, which were once the major reason to build a tiny house, are not the only reason anymore.

Reasons to build a tiny house:

They are cheaper to build and maintain. Hence, an individual facing an economic crisis may favor it over a huge house due to its affordability.

They are friendlier to the environment. Hence, it is considered a favorable alternative to huge houses for those who are keener on conserving the environment with their own actions.

Some individuals tend to find smaller spaces comforting and hence may prefer to live in a tiny house. It also lessens the responsibility around the house offering you a lesser work burden and more time for relaxation.

Certain individuals tend to live in huge houses especially when there are more members in the family. However, their children may move out after a certain age and hence they prefer to shift to a smaller space relevant to their needs. Tiny houses can serve as a good option.

Children who tend to move out at a certain age may want to buy their own place but have financial constraints. Tiny houses are ideal for them as spaces smaller than 1000 square feet are affordable and are an ideal size for solitary living. In addition, they offer you ample privacy in case you are living alone.

Uses of tiny houses:

Tiny houses can serve many more purposes than just little homes for you to live in. With time, people have improvised and come up with many uses for them. Architecture plays a huge role in these different uses as the way they are built can serve different purposes.

You may be perfectly comfortable living in your huge houses. However, you never know your need to build a tiny house for an all new purpose. Here are a few of the uses:

They can be built for your children close to your own house to facilitate them. This way your children can enjoy a personal set-up with their own privacy yet be facilitated by having their parent's house close by in case of need.

Some individuals prefer having their elderly people shifted to old age homes to allow themselves the privacy to their own homes etc. A tiny house serves the purpose as elderly people may not require a lot of space as they tone down to a simpler lifestyle.

You may set up your very own home office close by or even in your backyard if you happen to live in a huge area. This allows you many advantages such as reduced commuting time and money, the convenience of working close to home, lesser investment to set up your own office etc.

Guest houses can be built in the form of tiny homes which can allow visitors to enjoy maximum privacy while enjoying the comfort and feel of a real home. Many a times, families or a group of friends choose to travel together and prefer to live together. This set-up allows them to enjoy a decent set-up complete with the basic essentials.

Resorts may also be built under this concept next to beaches which offers a bigger attraction to tourists to relax with all the basic necessities. This is because in areas like these which are far away from main stores, a comfortable home type set-up with basic essentials can be quite attractive.

This concept can also be used to make homes for the homeless as they require lesser investment and the accommodation of more people in a decent enough set-up.

A dorm set-up may also use this concept. All the integral facilities may be provided in this case and students be allowed full privacy and a luxurious set-up at their disposal.

Chapter 4: Choose Your Space With Positivity And Practicality: Choice

Renovation and re-adjustment for every human being on the planet earth is difficult, as the earth itself is a tiny jug with a little liquid called atmosphere in it!

Moreover, that which, moves. Oh boy! It moves. We are nomads with not just one sense of sanity, but zillions!

This is why the emphasis should be slightly high on estimating the rate of how much there it is, to **be lived** rather than **to live**! In accordance to that, one should also comprehend positivity is one virtue that glides as a harbinger of comfort! And it also metamorphoses into Practicality. That is, what it is best for you is to survive! Our present progressive era tends to call the act not for survival, but 'to live'. Hence, the first lesson of de-cluttering, is make your habitat into a liveable tiny beauty nest called home!

Why de-clutter your space?

De-cluttering is neither the end of the world nor the elixir of **momentariness**. Rather, de-cluttering is necessary whenever you feel that breath of friction in your comfort orbit. When the dust has paid for your **no-sneeze** or **broom's volume**, make sure you do a **de-cluttering**. Although, de-cluttering is the starting step of cleaning, the primary goal lies in preparing yourself to a refreshing **slumber-after**.

To start with, there are many advantages of de-cluttering:

Making space

New arrangement

Discomfort in movement

Crowding

Shrinking

Audibility

Visibility and Light

Climatic changes

Occasion/ Event

Apart from the above, there are many more psychological and physical necessities to opt for de-cluttering, as it is not just for removal of certain items that you do this, but for a somersault all the way up and down the hill! Additionally, when you are light on 'your stuff on earth', as George Carlin says, it's the **ping to soar**! Simply put, you will have no trouble over shifting, moving or being subject to changes, which is what life is all about!

The major part of de-cluttering lies in the prime aspect of **when** you do it. As always, people have two ways of going over it. First is periodic. And the other is impulsive. The former advocates cleaning and waste management strategies that are taking place monthly, yearly or daily. While the latter dictates to clean whenever you realize your threshold of hygiene, that is, whenever you see congested space or realize having a feeling of such!

Spring cleaning or cleaning because of guests/events tends to be rather deep, thorough and precise, that de-cluttering, cleanliness and health becomes a part of our vitality to all movement and rest. Having the knowledge of **how to** will arm you to battle the rest of it. The forthcoming chapters provide the details of how to de-clutter your space, life and house to make a beautiful home out of it.

Briefly said, the how of this project is essential to determining the depth of the project so one must have a clear idea of what, why and what the rough average budget is he throwing away!

Yes, the catch of this action is precisely that.

What are you willing to throw away and perhaps earn a few bucks out of?

That being said let us move onto the basic preparation of how to start with de-cluttering.

Chapter 5: Planning For Your Tiny House

When you are designing your own tiny home, you will notice that the process is a little bit different compared to planning for a traditional-sized house. With a tiny home, one needs to keep the design more compact without sacrificing comfort.

Before starting to buy furniture and construct the walls of your new abode, you need to draft a plan first. With solid design tactics, you can address any problems that you may encounter during the construction phase. It will also help reduce costs because you already know how much space you will work on, and furniture and décor that you will buy. In this chapter, you will learn more about planning and design strategies that will help you create the most amazing tiny home that you can ever have.

How to Get Started?

1. Sketch it using the old-fashioned technique. In most cases, a good design concept starts by sketching it on paper. However, your drawing can become more useful when you do it to scale. This will allow you to have better understanding of each element in your tiny home.

To start sketching, grab a piece of graph paper that does not have an extremely dense grid. You can also print your own by downloading templates online. You can use a pen, marker and pencil for sketching.

The squares of the grid must be equal to a fraction of a foot. For example, a single square can measure six inches. After determining the equivalent of each square, multiply it by the other cells in your graph paper.

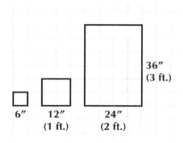

Using the sample equivalent (1 square = 6"), selecting 30 squares will equal to 180"or 15'. To compute for the feet measurement, just divide the inches by 12. If you are planning to grab a square table that measures 24", its representation on the graph paper is a 4 x 4 grid.

2. After drawing your concept on paper, you can redraw it using architecture software. The task may seem redundant, but these programs have advanced tools that will help you delve into the specific details of your tiny home floor plan. Professional designers mostly use AutoCAD for designing homes. However, you do not really need extremely serious and expensive software for this task. Even if you use a basic web-based design software, you can already create a floor plan that suits your need since there is only little space to work on.

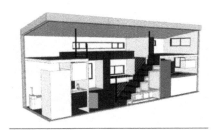

One of the platforms that you can use for home and interior design is SketchUp. It is a free 3D rendering software that caters to beginner-level designers. Using SketchUp, you can design your flooring and other important details of your home. Since you can render three dimensional models, you can easily visualize what it will look like when you start constructing it in real life.

In addition, you can also find a lot of tutorials online.

Determining the dimensions

1. When it comes to determining the size of your home, make sure to consider wall thickness. It can be difficult to know the exact dimensions of your wall, but you are free to make an estimate. A standard 2 x 4 stud wall lined with a drywall on both sides can measure around 4.5 inches thick.

2. Also, consider the size of your doors. Usually, doors can differ in width size and have 2"increments. A typical American

home usually has a front door that measures 3'wide and 7'tall. However, this one is too big for a tiny home. It is ideal to try the standard tiny home door size, which measures 2'9". When choosing a door, make sure that your largest furniture can fit through it.

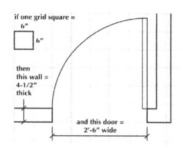

if one grid square = 6"

6"

then this wall = 4-1/2" thick

and this door = 2'-6" wide

3. Next, determine where you will place your windows. You have the freedom to determine the size of your window, but as mentioned in the previous chapter, it is ideal to install bigger ones to allow more natural light to enter your home.

4. Set realistic expectations when choosing furniture. Tiny homes have limited floor space, so make sure to select pieces of furniture that are suitable to your home.

5. For the kitchen dimensions, allot at least 36"of working space so that you can fit the cabinets or tables in your drawing.

6. For bathroom dimensions, you can refer to building codes in your area to get a good estimate. For starters, allot around 15"of space between the toilet and the wall.

Chapter 6: Design Ideas

Some people purchase floor plans from seasoned tiny house architects, while others are quite satisfied with the free ones they found on the internet. Naturally, you should take the "free" route first, but if nothing suits your fancy, then go for the professionally made one.

Nevertheless, regardless of whether you end up buying a plan or getting hands on with it, the following tips will help you carve out exactly what you want before you move on to the actual building process.

Sketch Out a Floor Plan

Drawing your floor plan to scale is essential and will require tools to be accurate with the overall layout, including the fixtures and furniture. To measure to scale, first draw out the maximum length and width that you have decided for your tiny house on graph paper.

Take note of the number of squares per inch on your graph paper. Next, count how many squares per length and width your graph paper has, then multiply them to know the total number of squares. Then, these limitations to determine how many squares will make up one square foot. Alternatively, use a digital application to sketch out your floor plan with ease.

Once you have prepared the tools, you can sketch out the exterior walls of your tiny house, taking into consideration their thickness. On average, the thickness is between 4 ½ to 6 ½ inches, so bring that to scale based on the measurements you have set.

Once you have your exterior walls, the next step is to determine where you want your door and window openings. This depends on the size of the doors and windows you have chosen. Most tiny house builders have already sourced these ahead of time to save on cost, and they even incorporate these materials' existing measurements as part of their floor plan. Windows are drawn as double lines, while doors are drawn as single line and sketched as fully opened with an arc. Make sure that your furniture can fit through the doors later on.

To design a floor plan, make a list of the major features that you want in your tiny house first. These include the kitchen, bath, toilet, living and/or work area, and sleeping area. After the doors and windows have been sketched in, you can then divide space among the different major features. Take into consideration the size and scope of the materials you will be installing there. In this case, you should know exactly what you want for each area. For instance, if you want to have a spacious kitchen, then you may want to dedicate the lion's share in square feet to it. However, if you also want to put a tub in the bathroom, then that means you will need to make some adjustments.

Keep in mind that the loft area is not a part of this limitation and is often used as the sleeping area. Determine the amount of headroom you are comfortable with on the loft and find a design that will not cause you to hunch over and feel cramped.

Once you have allocated the different spaces in your tiny house, you should then determine the length and width of the built-in fixtures for them, starting from the kitchen and bath. Find out where you can get miniaturized versions of sinks and if you can trim down regular countertops to save on space. Refurbished sinks, toilets, gas ranges, and other appliances from RVs, for instance, are great built-in fixtures for tiny houses.

Get Creative with the Design

When planning on the design of your tiny house, don't forget to consider the climate and seasons in your residential site. If you are going to live in a place with extreme weather conditions, then you should prioritize the heating and cooling system. Air flow into and out of the house should be part of the design as well, especially if you do not want to turn your little home into an oven. Also, make sure that your house will not come crumbling down if your location is susceptible to heavy rains, snowstorms, or the occasional hail.

The next step in the design process is to decide on your house "theme." Some factors to consider are the location of your tiny house, the size of it, the materials you will be using, and of course, your lifestyle. There are tiny houses that have a cozy, log cabin feel to them, build mostly out of wood and unpainted to the appeal of the natural look. There are modernized ones that use shipping containers and incorporate more glass and metal, reflecting a minimalistic, urban lifestyle. There are interesting, eccentric houses that show a more charming, albeit unusual, vibe. These are oftentimes made out salvaged materials that dramatically reduce the overall cost.

The most obvious challenge when it comes to designing your tiny house is the use of space. Nobody wants to feel claustrophobic, even if your tolerance for small spaces is high. Space efficiency is crucial, so make your rooms and furniture multi-purpose and do not neglect the use of outdoor space as well. Sliding walls, instead of doors, work great in tiny homes because these remove the "swinging space" consumed by regular doors. Instead of solid walls, consider curtain room dividers within your tiny house, and unless you have a thing for kitschy designs, keep everything clean and simple!

Tiny House, Big Space Ideas

The ability to make your tiny house not feel so cramped is an art form in and of itself. If you are not yet sure on how to make your tiny house look big and airy, then here are some great suggestions that you can incorporate into your design:

Install glass doors and large windows.

Glass doors and large windows will allow natural light to come in and reduce your use of energy. You also allow the outdoors to be more visible indoors, which will keep the tiny house from feeling boxed in.

Use light-colored, if not white, paint.

Light colors absorb more light and give the room an overall spacious feel. Choose soft colors to add a bit of personality to your space, such as pastels. Dark colors are also wonderful as long as they are present on accent pieces. You can also choose a monochromatic palette (such as using your favourite color, but in different shades) to give the space an overall uniform look, as opposed to the crowded feeling caused by a plethora of colors.

Opt for multi-purpose and space saving furniture.

You will find plenty of multi-purpose appliances and furniture nowadays. The most common are the convertible sofa beds, the ottoman chairs that can be used as storage boxes, the fold-down table, stackable tables and chairs, staircases that double as storage space, and much more. You can either buy the stuff or install them as part of the tiny house itself.

Install shelves close to the ceiling.

As much as possible, keep the floor bare. That is why, in a tiny house, vertical storage is key. Open shelves hung near the ceiling are preferred by most tiny house owners for two main reasons. First, it allows them to access items quickly without having to swing open cabinet doors. Second, it forces them to see exactly how many items they keep on the shelves, thereby compelling them to pare down on their possessions once things start to get cluttered.

Choose one major piece instead of several small ones.

A small space will look much more put together if there is one large piece of furniture in it rather than several small ones that will make it look cluttered. It also helps to choose pieces with exposed legs because these can provide more floor space. On top of that, it makes cleaning the floor so much easier.

When in doubt, use glass and Lucite materials.

Glass and Lucite materials will not only let more light into the room, but also make the space look a whole lot more streamlined. They are also a fool-proof way to make your tiny house look absolutely modern and minimalistic.

Use mirrors as accent pieces.

A sure-fire way to make your tiny house look big is to use mirrors. They reflect light and the room back, making the space look so much bigger.

There are plenty of other ideas and designs that you can look into. Devour every single piece of free information you can find online and in books, then use those to create the best possible tiny house design that your budget and resources will allow. All of the time and effort that you will put into your design will lead to the kind of results that will truly speak to your heart.

Chapter 7: Downsizing Within Reason

The greatest benefit of going tiny is gaining a mortgage free life. But, there are challenges to keeping your life free of any mortgage payment. The first challenge is "going tiny." Yes, it is a benefit, but it is also a challenge because you have to learn to live in a space that may be a quarter, a half, or three-quarters of the home size you are used to. There are certain rules that will make the choice to downsize easier.

The Right Size

Numerous studies have been conducted by experts on how much space the average American needs to feel comfortable in their home. These experts state that 100 sq. feet per person is the smallest amount of space the average person can live in. If you have four people in your family, you need at least 400 square feet for your home. Ideally, 500 square feet is better, so you have 100 sq. feet of community space.

Every person, no matter how close a family they are, needs time to themselves. It is not reasonable to expect that the great outdoors will always be able to provide you the space you need away from others. Freezing cold temperatures, where frostbite happens in seconds, if you go outside can hinder your "space." Temperatures in the 90s to 100s, or higher can lead to heat stroke. Thunderstorms with lightning, hurricanes, or tornadoes can also prevent you from going outside. Yes, these storms do not last, but what if you are cooped up for 3 days? Can you survive if you only have 10 sq. feet per person?

Most people find that sometimes there is such a thing as too tiny. The right size is all about knowing yourself first, and then knowing the other people you are going to live with, in your tiny home. If you are a married couple, with no plans for children in the next five years, then you may feel comfortable with only 200 sq. feet. But, what happens if birth control did not do its job, and you have a baby before you planned? Can you live in 200 sq. feet with a baby or for those five years before you can afford a larger home for your growing family?

The situations mentioned and questions asked do not mean you are going to answer the same way as the next person that reads this book. Rather, you are thinking about the "what ifs" and determining who you are as a person.

For example, one person interested in building a tiny house is comfortable living in a small amount of space, without anyone else living in that same space. However, this person knows that there is a need for high ceilings. An eight-foot-high ceiling is not enough, despite being just over 5 feet, eight feet high ceilings makes this person feel closed in. If there is not at least 4 to 5 feet of floor space running from the front to the back of the tiny house, without walls, the person also feels closed in. If you know things like this about yourself, then you can either plan to build a home that fits your quirks or you can immediately know that tiny house living is not for you.

Vehicle and Trailer Costs

The discussion on size must include the two options you have for building your tiny house: trailer or fixed home. A trailer can affect your downsizing benefits. Have you watched some of the tiny home shows on TV? Several people have built their home for $10,000 or $20,000 on trailers, but was the show specific? Did the show state the cost to build the house was $10,000 and this included the trailer? Most are ambiguous on this point. Typically, the shows are all about how much the materials, furniture, and labor costs were for building the house, but don't actually include the cost of the vehicle or trailer you need for towing your tiny house.

The next cardinal rule for reducing your monetary constraints is knowing what the vehicle and trailer will cost you in addition to the building materials.

Each vehicle and trailer has a GVWR or gross vehicle weight rating. It can also be called the GVM or gross vehicle mass. This is the safe operating weight/mass your vehicle can have. It includes the vehicle chassis, body, engine, engine fluids, fuel, accessories, driver, cargo, and passengers. For the trailers, it includes the chassis, axles, floor of the trailer, and all other trailer components.

Let's say you have a truck that says it has 6,200 pound GVWR, and the vehicle weighs 5,000 pounds. What do you think you can safely carry inside the vehicle? If you said 1,200 pounds, then you are correct. If you add a 300-pound tongue weight trailer, then the amount decreases to 900 pounds for the vehicle. So, including passengers and what you carry in the actual vehicle, you can carry 900 pounds, with a trailer.

The truck has to be able to tow the trailer size you want to have based on towing capacity and GVWR. Most ¾ ton or 1 ton trucks can pull the maximum trailer size for tiny homes.

Most states allow you to have up to 60 feet with a truck/trailer length. You may be able to drive an RV that is towing a vehicle and be up to 65 feet in length. For a trailer and motor home situation, which is the closest to a tiny house set up, you can be up to 45 feet in length, with a maximum height of 13 feet 6 inches.

Now, you understand the background information. It is time to discuss the costs. For a brand new 1-ton truck with a hemi and heavy duty rating, which is required for pulling the largest tiny house size, you would need to spend anywhere from $50,000 to $75,000 for the vehicle. If you are willing to fix up a used vehicle, you may be able to find an HD hemi 1-ton truck for $25,000 to $40,000.

Certain online tiny house retailers sell trailers for a maximum of $7,000, which is their 26-foot trailer. Other places may require up to $10,000 for a trailer that is set up for tiny house creations. You can also spend as little as $1,000 for a trailer, where you may need to spend a little more adding axles and welding the bolts to the trailer to secure the frame of your tiny house.

Let's say you are going for the larger tiny house, thus you need at least $50,000 for the newer vehicle and $7,000 for the 26-foot trailer. Already, you have spent $57,000 for the tiny house, without factoring in the building costs. Will this get you away from a mortgage or loan?

You might need an auto loan to fund your traveling tiny house, which may not bring you any further ahead financially. Remember that most auto loans are paid off in 5 years or less, thus your monthly car payment can be extremely large.

Now, if you already have a vehicle that can tow the trailer or already bought a trailer, these costs could ensure you get away from borrowing money from a bank. Everyone's situation is different. It is just a consideration you have to make when determining if you can stick with the cardinal rule of not having any type of loan at all to create your tiny house.

Land Costs

The thought that a tiny house is more affordable when it is not fixed to a piece of land can be somewhat of a myth depending on where you want to live. Obviously, some individuals want the mobility of a tiny house, but if you have no intentions of traveling then you may be better off finding a land deal.

Although rare, there are still some states in the USA that offer cheap land. It may not be in the most glamorous of locations, but if you work from home like many traveling tiny home owners—it may not matter where you live.

The downside is if you want to live in the city, such as New York, New Orleans, or other big cities, you may be right back to paying a mortgage for 200 sq. feet. Some tiny homes have sold for $250,000 to be in downtown New York, Charleston, or New Orleans.

There is one rule of owning land that can be appealing to tiny home owners. Land accrues equity, rather than depreciating like a vehicle and trailer. Land when it has a home on it, has more value. If you spend $50,000 on a piece of land and $10,000 to build your home, then you have at least

$60,000 in value. The key, of course, is being able to find the right situation.

Land can also help you reduce current mortgage costs. You may not be entirely mortgage free for 10 years, but you would have a lower mortgage than if you purchased land with 2,000 square foot new construction built on it.

If you want to downsize to avoid high mortgages or any mortgage at all, then you will need to be savvy in your exploration for land. You could also approach friends or family that own land. You may be able to get 1 acre to build your home on for a reasonable value, if you know someone with land to spare.

An important rule is to go with what is most affordable as a means of avoiding the mortgage you ordinarily need for a home.

AvoidExpensive Tastes

Tiny houses do not have to be expensive, but they can certainly be unaffordable. One family built a tiny vacation home for $125,000. The home was around 200 square feet. This family wanted only the best in construction and technology. They wanted a tiny smart home, with a long granite countertop, wireless technology, and much more.

Your expensive tastes will increase the bill. This next rule asks you to think about what is most important to you, so you can avoid the mortgage or loan most homeowners end up with. It is also about making sure you do not blow the budget you have and spend more of your savings than you allot for the project.

If you want a full size fridge because you do not want to visit the store every two or three days, what are you willing to sacrifice in order to afford the appliance? When it comes to your bathroom vanity are you willing to spend $500 or can you make do with buying material for $60 and building your own vanity? To keep costs low and yourself mortgage free, you must be willing to compromise and sacrifice certain things you may desire.

Downsizing Steps

Determine your comfort level.

Examine your true self for space needs.

Do you need a land to accommodate your space requirements?

What is your budget?

Once steps 1 through 4 have answers, you may begin designing and planning for your tiny house.

Chapter 8: Basics Of Tiny House Living

Imagine living a simple life free of mortgage and rent in a little house that contains all that you need to live a comfortable life. The ever changing economic environment in the world is forcing many people to reevaluate how they live. Because of the recent economic troubles in the world especially the recent recession in the U.S. that resulted in many people falling behind in mortgage payment or losing their homes, many people are now considering adopting life in small houses that they can build on their tracks or in small space. Because of this, the United States is being swept by the tiny house movement.

Tiny house living is about living a simple and beautiful life in a tiny home with everything you need and with freedom from economic pressures associated with rent and mortgage payment of a conventional home. What is maybe considerably more essential than the economic benefits of owning a tiny home is the environmental advantages. Living in a Tiny House conveys a much smaller ecological impact, decreases the number of appliances you need to live and encourages you to consume less. These lifestyle adjustments greatly help conserve the environment.

So what exactly is a Tiny House?

There are no industry measures to decide when a house is viewed as tiny. A space that may be viewed as "tiny" for a group of four could be large for a single individual family. In the recent times, there have been efforts by a number of groups to contribute to the definition of the tiny house. The Small Housing Society established following the growth of the tiny house movement, has destinations for nine types of tiny houses. From a proficiency house of roughly 480 sq.ft. to a simple micro house which scarcely surpasses 160 sq.ft. The Society inclines towards what most North Americans would consider smaller spaces. A research on small houses in British Columbia Canada defines tiny homes of any structure (flat, disconnected homes or moveable unit) that is meant to meet the needs of its inhabitants' with minimal space, more particularly, roughly 500 sq.ft. For 1-2 individuals, or somewhat bigger at 750 sq.ft. For a family of 3 or more.

The Benefits of a Tiny House

There are many benefits that both you and the society can gain from tiny home living. When you live in a tiny house you will

have fewer appliances, consume less and thus reduce your bills. Smaller homes also are less expensive to build and maintain and thus saves you a lot of money. The following are some of the major benefits you will enjoy from living in a tiny house

You can move your home

Most tiny homes are built on trucks and fitted with solar panels and rainwater collection equipment. This makes the home movable and thus gives the benefits of moving around with your home. If yours is one of these then when you are tired of living in a given place all you need is to hitch your home to a truck and move it to a new location. If you are in college or you move from one town to the other more regularly especially if you are still single or haven't settled down in life then this is the perfect home for you. This is because when it is time to move you don't have to struggle packing suitcases or hiring a moving company to help you move. When you have to move you just hitch you home on a truck and move it to your new location.

It is relatively cheap to build and own

A tiny house is much smaller than the ordinary home and thus requires fewer materials and labor to build. In addition, it requires less space or you may simply build one on your truck. This greatly reduces the cost of buying land and putting up the home. In total building, a tiny home will cost you only a fraction of what you need to buy or build a normal size home. It is thus quite economical to won one.

It is environmentally friendly

A tiny home requires less wood to build and occupies less space than the conventional homes. This is a plus to the environment and fewer trees are cut down to produce the timber and there is more space for plants. In addition living in a tiny home means that you will consume less which in turn helps save the environment as most of what is consumed in homes come from the environment.

It is energy efficient

A tiny home will have fewer electrical appliances and thus consumes less energy than a conventional home. In addition being a smaller home, you don't need a lot of energy to hit up the home. This means that your power bill will be greatly reduced.

It is easy to clean

With less space, you don't have a lot of cleaning to do. In fact, cleaning will take you just a few minutes of dusting and sweeping. You can also easily de-clutter the house which makes cleaning even easier. So if you are not a fun of cleaning the living in a tiny home will be a big plus for you.

The Tiny House Movement

The tiny house movement is a social movement that has been advocating for simple living in tiny homes for the past few years. The movement encourages people worldwide to live in homes of about 500 square feet and below to help gain economic freedom and save the environment.

The history of the tiny house movement can be traced back to 1997 when Sarah Susanka published her book: The Not So Big House although there had been a number of early advocators for the tiny house living such as Lester Walker who published the book Tiny Houses in 1897 and Lloyd Kahn who authored the shelter in 1973. The idea of tiny houses on wheels was made popular by Jay Shafer who lived in a tiny house on a truck and also started two tiny house companies the Four Lights Tiny House Company and the Tumbleweed Tiny House Company.

In the United States, the tiny house movement began to grow in 2005 following the Hurricane Katrina when Marianne Cusato designed tiny homes on wheels for disaster prone areas and many people got interested in the idea. When the 2007/2008 many people lost jobs, businesses collapsed and quite a number of Americans lost their homes and much more could not pay their mortgage. This attracted the attention of more Americans to the tiny house movement. Today more and more people in America are trying to get into tiny homes due to their great economic and environmental benefits.

The tiny homes movement is active mainly in the United States. But it is important to note that there has been an increase in small house living in many other countries such as Japan, Spain, Britain, and Germany among others. The increase in tiny housing living in the world in the recent past means that more and more people are considering tapping into the benefit that tiny houses offers.

Factors to Consider Before Deciding to Move to a Tiny House

Today many of the advocates of tiny housing living encourage others to take the step and move into a small home so that they can focus on building their wealth and experiences. Well, moving into a tiny home many not always be smooth for everyone. Before you move to a tiny home consider the following important factors:

☐What is your goal for moving to a tiny house?

Before moving to a tiny house you need to consider your reasons for moving. This will help you settle down faster and feel comfortable in such a small space. For example, if your goal of opting to live in a tiny house is to save money, then you will have to sell a lot of your personal items so that you can trim your possessions to fit in a tiny home. So before you move consider your goals carefully and look for alternatives so that you don't feel like you are inconveniencing yourself by living in a tiny house when you finally make the move.

Location of your tiny home

The location is important when moving to a tiny home. You need to build your tiny home in the right location. If you are building your tiny home on wheels then you need to know where you will be parking your home. As you decide to move consider the available locations and see if you fit in well with your goals.

☐What kind of a tiny home you want?

Do you want to move into a permanent tiny home build on a foundation or do you prefer a home on wheels? If your reason for opting for a tiny home is the flexibility it offers when it comes to moving around then go for a tiny home on wheels. If you don't move around a lot then a tiny home with a permanent foundation is perfect for you.

☐Decide on the size of the home based on your lifestyle and family size

Your lifestyle will determine how many things you need to live in comfort. This will, in turn, determine the minimum space you need to be comfortable. For example, if you love to play music, watch TV and play video games then you may need space for such activities this will mean that you need a little bit more space than an individual who is more interested in just a places to sleep and have some private time. If you have a family of four then your space need may be more than that of a family of two.

Before you Move, Try

Starting life in a tiny house may be quite challenging especially if you are used to leaving in a larger home. So if you are thinking of building or buying your own tiny house make an effort to try living in such a small space so that you know if you will be comfortable. You can rent a vacation cabin and see how your life will be like living in a small space.

Outdoor space is always important

When you live in a small house you have limited space and that is when outdoor decks and porches become important. So when deciding on your tiny home needs fact in the outdoor space. This will help give you more comfortable.

☐Plan how you will get your utilities

If you want to live in a tiny home on wheels then you should plan how you will get clean water, electricity and sewage disposal services. You may use solar panels for electricity but you will still need to plan how you will dispose of wastes and how you will get your water and other utilities.

Start Living in a Tiny House

Living in a small house for the first time is not always easy for many people. You thus need to prepare well before moving into a tiny house. Follow these simple steps to start living in a tiny house:

☐Do research on what you need in a tiny house

Tiny houses come in various shapes and sizes. Before you move you need to know what exactly you need in a tiny house. What kind of space do you need, what form of design do you need and how do you want to your home set. This is important as it will help prepare you for what you are getting into.

☐Decide to build or buy a tiny house

Once you know the kind of a small house that you need the next step is to decide if you are buying or building one. If you own a plot of land or you have a truck you may decide to build your own tiny house. This will save you a lot of money as you get to do most of the work. However, you may also find it right to buy an already build tiny house. This is the first step to moving to your own tiny house.

☐Cut down your belongings

Quite often we use less than 20% of our personal effects regularly. Sort out your household items and sell off those that you really don't need and sell or give them away. This will help reduce the number household items you have to only those you will need in a tiny house. You may also consider selling some of your larger appliances and replace them with smaller once. For example, if you have a larger Fridge, TV or cooker you may consider swapping it for a smaller one.

☐Practice leaving in a tiny house

To comfortably shift to a tiny house you need to start practicing living in a tiny house. Once you buy a small house or you start building your own you may start preparing and yourself and your family for life in a tiny house. you can make it progressive over several months for example if you live in a large house, you may start by moving to a one bedroom apartment then as you adjust to that space you move to a tiny travel cabin where you will leave for a number of months so that you adjust your life. This is important as it helps you withdraw from electronics controlled life and gives a great mindset to start life in your own tiny house.

☐Move to Your own tiny house

This is the last step to living in your own tiny house. Once you have adjusted your life to living in a tiny house and you have cut down on your belonging and you have acquired your tiny house you now move to your permanent address. Here you plan and arrange your home and start your life. At first, you may not have all that you need to live in comfort. Be on the lookout for what you can do to improve your living in such a tiny space. Be open to new ideas and plan to make changes regularly as this will make your life more interesting.

Strategies for Adapting to Life in a Small

To successfully live in a tiny home you need to consider a number of strategies. This is important because quite often a small house will have less space and you will find it difficult bring in new things or doing a lot of other things that you can do in a conventional large house. The following are important strategies that you should consider:

☐ Cut down on entertainment

Watching TV and playing computer games is an important part of modern day lifestyle. Entertainment means that you have to buy more appliances for such gratification which in the long run will eat up space for other important things. To be comfortable and reduce the urge to buy more entertainment gadgets reducing entertainment to watching public TV and playing games on your Smartphone online. Instead focus more on outdoor activities. This will help make your life healthier and more fulfilling.

☐Adopt the one in one out strategy

Due to space constraints that come with living in a tiny house ensure that whenever you buy something big for your home, you take out something that occupies the same space. This is an important strategy that will ensure you maintain a balance in the space in your home. For example, whenever you buy new clothes you may consider donating some of your older once.

☐Put to use any free space

Consider buying new furniture and appliances for your tiny house that make effective use of space. For example, go for furniture that has inbuilt closed storage compartments. This will help with storing your belongings and thus reduce clutter and keep your small house organized. Also, build storage compartments in free spaces along the walls to help with storage of your other belongings so as to help keep your home organized and increase space.

☐ Make the interior of your home attractive

Carefully work on the layout and decoration of your tiny home to make it attractive. This is important as it will make your home more appealing to you and thus give you more comfort. You may use colors to make your home appear larger and thus attractive to the eye.

Living in a tiny house takes a lot of flexibility and creativity on your part. There is no standard rule to living in a tiny house. You need to use your creativity and ingenuity to make your tiny house both attractive and comfortable. Once you decide to move to a tiny home study how you can improve your life while living in such a home and work on it. Be open to learning new things and use your creativity to make your life more comfortable.

Chapter 9: The Benefits Of Living In A Tiny House

Living in a tiny house brings a host of benefits to individuals and families who chose to make this change.

Less Cost

One of the main benefits that anyone can enjoy from transitioning to the tiny lifestyle is the freedom from debt. Although this does not happen instantly, downsizing is the most important step to achieving financial independence. As discussed in the previous chapter, living in tiny houses can reduce not just the cost of building a house, but its maintenance and upkeep as well. In fact, studies show that 68% of folks who live in tiny houses have no mortgages.

When there is less money spent on maintaining the home, families can start saving for things that matter more, such as college education and retirement.

Improved Relationships

Space can, of course, be a good thing. However, too much of it in a home can result to family members drifting apart. It is quite common for the entire family to be at home, but often be in separate rooms. This usually leads to children feeling distant from parents or couples not being able to communicate well with each other. Eventually, these will have unpleasant consequences.

Tiny houses give the family time to bond without compromising privacy. Since these homes are designed to fit the needs of the family, each member can still have his or her own space but still be close to each other.

Less Waste

Having a smaller environmental footprint is one of the focal points of tiny living. Naturally you have less waste because you occupy a much smaller space. You can also choose to go green by opting for an off-the-grid design. By using compost toilets and recycling grey water, you can help protect and sustain the environment.

In addition, occupying less space means there is more land for other environmentally and economically friendly ideas which can include urban farming or gardening.

Improved Finances

The cost of building and maintaining a tiny house is considerably less than what it would cost for a traditional sized home. You also do not need to get a loan that will take forever to pay off because you will be spending less. In fact, 78% of people who live in tiny houses own their homes and most are mortgage-free. This is an impressive number in comparison to the 29% of traditional homeowners.

Most American families live on credit which can be disastrous when finances start to get shaky. This is what happened in the 2007 financial crisis when families lost their homes because they could no longer make their mortgage payments. Building and living in their dream homes turned into a nightmare.

By choosing to go tiny, individuals and families can live comfortably, but not excessively. This ensures that there is money saved for rainy days.

Chapter 10: Building A Tiny House

Many people are encouraged to build tiny houses because of the many benefits that it can give. However, there are some things that you need to consider when it comes to building a tiny house. This chapter will highlight all there is to know about building a tiny house.

Things to Consider When Building a Tiny House

Building a tiny house is as challenging as building a conventional house. There are several things that need to be considered when it comes to building a tiny house. Below are the factors that you need to consider when it comes to building a tiny house:

Cost

There are many anecdotal references that indicate that those who own tiny homes spend between $15,000 and $25,000 on complete homes. However, those who hire professional builders to construct their tiny homes might need to spend between $30,000 and $50,000 depending on the complexity of the design. Other people spend more than $50,000 to build their tiny homes. It is important to take note that just because tiny houses are small does not mean that you can spend less. It is crucial for you to prepare the right amount to fund the construction of your tiny home. The purpose of building a tiny house is to save money thus it is important that you keep up with this goal by designing a tiny house that will fit within your allowed budget.

Types of Tiny Houses

Tiny houses can exist in different shapes, sizes and forms. In fact, you can build tiny houses from sheds, barns or cabins. Some people have also made tiny houses using trailer vans, RVs or tree houses. You can also buy pre-planned designs of tiny homes from the internet. Your options when it comes to building a tiny house is limitless as you can build a house on pre-existing structures or build one from new materials. The thing is that there is no standard design of tiny houses and you can become as creative as you can when designing tiny homes. What matters is that you consider the functionality of your house.

Location

Another factor that you need to consider when building a tiny house is the location. The best thing about tiny house living is that you are not limited to building your house on a piece of land. You can design it as a tree house or as a moving trailer house. What you need to do is to figure out what type of tiny house you would like to live in. It is also crucial to take note that the design of your tiny house should also complement the location where you want to build your house.

Permits

Although tiny houses especially built on a trailer falls under the category of a travel trailer, there are many tiny houses that are immobile or built on a small area of land. Technically, a tiny house that is a size of shed does not need any construction permits but it may not also be considered as a legal dwelling place in many states. It is always important to check with the local planning department in your area before you build your tiny house and get the necessary permits.

How to Build a Tiny House

Before you start designing your tiny house, it is important that you learn how to build a tiny house. The process of building a tiny house is similar to building a big house. However, the difference is that a tiny house would require you to focus on areas of the house that are truly necessary. Below are the steps to building a tiny house that you can also call home.

Design the Tiny House

When designing a tiny house, it is important that you keep the design of the building simple. It is necessary that you avoid complicated walls, wide windows and other excessive ornamental features in your home. Every space of a tiny house should be functional so adding excessive elements on your design will not only make your tiny house less efficient but also more costly. There are many types of design that you can use as a reference when building a tiny house. Below is a list of three types of foundation that you can adapt when building a tiny house:

Tiny House on a Trailer

This is the most common type of tiny house that people build. As the name implies, it is a house built on a trailer van thus its size is no wider than 8 feet and no taller than 13.5 feet. This is a great option for single people or couples but it is also good for a growing family. In most cases, a tiny house on a trailer comes with RV hookups thus making this house a great alternative to conventional RVs. When designing a tiny house on a trailer, make sure that it is road worthy.

Ground Bound Houses

Ground bound houses are constructed on a read foundation such as a slab or on the ground. The benefit of this particular design is that conventional utilities can run to the house aside from setting up off-grid facilities such as a rainwater collection tank, solar panel cells and a composting toilet. Another great advantage for this particular tiny house design is that it offers you freedom of shape, size as well as height of your home. Examples of ground-bound houses include cottages, cabins and barns. Tree houses, on the other hand, are also considered under category especially if they have permanent structures that are connected to the ground such as the stairs.

Hybrid Portable Houses

Hybrid portable houses are considered as one of the most versatile as well as flexible types of tiny houses. This type of house looks like a ground bound house but wheels can be attached to it. This means that it can be moved like a trailer house but it can also rest on a semi-permanent foundation. This is a perfect house for people who cannot decide which type of tiny house they want to live in.

When deciding the design of the tiny house, it is crucial that you consider your preferences. As a house owner, ask yourself what kind of living would like to have?

Build the Foundation

When building a tiny house, it is important that you first build the foundation of your house. The material that is easiest to use when it comes to building tiny houses is wood. Wood boards are preferred when it comes to building tiny houses is that it is lightweight and versatile. Moreover, should you want to make changes in your house in the future, you can easily undertake the renovations by yourself if you use wood.

Prepare the Utilities

The utilities inside a tiny house are quite different compared to those found in conventional homes. In most cases, tiny houses are run on off-grid technologies which means that these homes do not rely on the connection of power, gas and water lines for comfort. In fact, most tiny houses are also not connected to the sewage system thus they have to be designed in such a way that they are sufficient in producing their own energy and water as well as deal with wastes.

Some alternative options that owners of tiny homes use include solar panel cells to produce their own electricity, rain water collecting tanks to harvest rain water and a composting toilet to deal with wastes. Make sure that you also design proper wiring and plumbing to compliment any alternative systems that you are going to adapt for your tiny house. Thus, when you are planning to build your very own tiny house, it is important that you consider these things and incorporate them in your design.

Weather-Proof Your House

Another important thing that you need to consider when designing your tiny house is to weather-proof it. Make sure that you wrap the floors and walls with a breathable material to keep it dry as well as protected from the elements. And since tiny houses have limited in space, most tiny house owners also face the problem of insulating their homes. It is therefore crucial for you to put insulation for your tiny house. Using a foam board is a common way to insulate your house but you can also use other materials as well.

What is important is to look for a material that can stop radiant heat as well as air leaks so that you can regulate the temperature in your home well. Make sure that you insulate not only your walls but also your floor and also roof.

FinishEverything Up

Once the major construction elements are done, the last step in the process is to finish everything up. Make sure that finish the interior trims as well as paint on both the interior and exterior of your tiny house. You can finally move in once you are finished with the painting.

Building a tiny house is a very exciting task and you don't need a lot of time and effort to finish this project. In fact, you can work on it every weekend and you can finish the project within a few months' time depending on the size of the house and if you have someone to help you finish the project.

Chapter 11: Utilizing The Space Available If You Live In A Small Home

How can you provide visitors you'd need to have people over to get a meal and if you stay in a little degree? If you not have adequate room to get a stay the choice you've prepared to take your dinner is being consumed by you from your legs, that'snot really attractive to friends. The other choice you've could be to get yourself a sofa table, sofa that folds out in to a table, not very useless really.

Anyone that's previously been on the vacation in even a caravan or a motorhome automobile may remember the sofa table, a remarkably uncomfortable "patch together" lounge that's made out of the table top turning to provide the foundation for your chair. The older and a lot more authentic types of these couches used to develop your feet feel useless in the legs down after being lay for worthwhile amount of time to them. Luckily, have shifted the sofa table and instances because of research, design and technology has become a reasonably comfortable furniture item.

Using the prices of property and property growing continuously many first time clients are experiencing to remain for really little box-type flats or properties that not leave much room for fantastic furniture, with all of the improvement in the sofa table they're currently able to have a greater habitable area in their homes together with possess some excellent furniture to proceed inside their homes.

Because of the increase in the amount of smaller properties that purchased and are now being purchased several house artist brands have become involved in production and developing furniture specially for this field of business. No more have you got to maintain with cheap furniture that's poorly-made to enter your really small hotel, now you might have artist-quality through your home.

Lounge tables are available in designs and many tones to match all interior design variations, buying one of the furnishings does not imply that you'll have to enhance your whole hotel to get the furniture to match. Towards the alternative these things are ready to mix in precisely with many people and many interior design models would not even know the distinction between a sofa table along with a regular lounge. The something missing in the room will be the table.

Every possible product type can be acquired to get a sofa table. You could have leather, that's how practical the choice is in addition to organic cotton, used gingham, crushed velvet, linen, tweed. That's an operating touch of contemporary furniture. If by any chance you Can't find shade or the design of sofa table that you need you could reduce of obtaining one the street, especially created with a custom for you. The result goes to be just what you needed to get into your house, though this can charge more money to have one created to your right format. It's an incredibly common method of getting the proper lounge although the cost might be prohibitive. So there you've it in conclusion, you might have the furniture youare looking for really small house. The sofa table, little, practical and fashionable.

When you stay in a little property where space is fixed an assortment of techniques 'll probably try to develop your living area seem bigger than its. Here is the concept behind the employment of strategically placed mirrors. Place on a big mirror because of the reflected a wall being created from that representation and, light, you realize a larger feeling of detail. The same concept happens when you work with a glass coffeetable, or perhaps an extremely slick or lacquered floor - light is found down, back in the region, making it appear larger. Include the sensation, crystal glass ornaments and, again of space is increased. Moreover, you can buy paint that, when positioned on your walls, offers a reflective surface. The general use of each of these home room- some substantial approaches might transfer to developing a small house appear to be bigger.

Now you've arranged the fabric it is time to complete some detail. Despite widespread perception, the correct use of several big furnishings may actually reduce the impact of dust. Creating full use of these reflective characteristics of color and other accessories along with a variety of large furnishings can give your location an appropriate, peaceful part while if youare to change these few big furniture products with smaller furnishings the appearance of the region is enhanced completely to 1 of pokiness - the wonder is lost. Allow any stunning photographs, take advantage of varied designs including silk velour velvet and cambric cambric, collections or plaids provide answer to simple materials in for function and, natural shades.

The total importance of house space-saving ideas is on applying the total amount of light going around for light to become proven off your different reflective materials that light needs to find a way to enter the space and, the room. Replace heavy curtains with lighting, airy materials for instance complete voiles - perhaps with embroidered detail to add interest. The basic effect is just a light, fashionable region that delivers comfort and cozy intimacy. Following on with all of the design of house space-saving tips take a look in the most recent in Futon sofa convertibles. These innovative Futon designs may perform a lot to contribute towards the beauty of the newly created small living area and, if required, following through with property space-saving ideas, these Futon sofas convert into a guest bed.

Actually, one of the best ideas I Have noticed to get an extended-time comes in the form of the Futon sofa convertible that changes into bunkbeds - the start of the sofa becomes one-bed as the chair of the lounge becomes the following garbage. I am not pretending that particular design isn't extremely expensive - it is not at all a cheap option - nevertheless the concept behind the appearance is sound and, with regards to home space-saving ideas, this design is wholly amazing and complete fills whatever you'd expect from the sofa convertible.

Chapter 12: Hacks For Extending A Small House

While you can never depend upon the weather conditions, you do know to a certain extent what kind of weather you are likely to get if you build your tiny home in an area you know. The outside area of the home is vital to your living space. For example, you may want to **incorporate a deck** and can even come up with ideas of protecting the deck in the event of bad weather.

Having the living space leading directly to the deck helps because people sitting within the lounge area and on the deck can mingle easily, spreading the space so that it is more comfortable. In this case, a **simple shade canopy** has been used to keep the sun off guests although this can be made more substantial in bad weather areas.

Have you ever worried about how the smells of cooking will affect small home living? Well, aside from making sure that there is adequate ventilation, how about incorporating an outdoor kitchen?

With all the money you will be saving on mortgage payments, you may even want a top of the range kitchen but you don't have to go to these extremes. There are more modest kitchen appliances on the market that will do just as good a job.

No room to **incorporate your shower**? How about this for a hack? What you have to take into account is adequate drainage and anyone can learn that. It's not rocket science and if it frees up space for your day to day living, then it has to be an improvement on your life. Yes, of course, many small house owners have incorporated a shower room, but if you don't have the plumbing expertise and don't want condensation problems, this is the ideal solution. This shower stall gives the owner somewhere to change and also houses the laundry basket, making it a great addition to the small home. It is adequately private and you may even find that your skin gets softer absorbing the fresh air.

Tiny homes mean compromise in some ways, but on the other hand you get to play around with your own living space and are not confined to thinking in a set way. You can become the architect of your own life and have the freedom to incorporate all kinds of inventive ideas that the basic home doesn't allow you to.

The other thing that tiny homeowners enthuse about is having the time to be inventive because there is not so much housework needed. If you plan your home so that everything has its place and its function, then life gets considerably easier. Want to go to sleep looking at the stars? The sky is your limit and when you start to look into tiny home living, you begin to see so many possibilities that may not have occurred to you before. This is your chance to live life as you want to live it and keep your salary for things that matter rather than obligations that push you into a corner each month.

There are other ways that you can extend your home to give you more sleeping space, get creative. Use removable hammocks that can be hung from trees in your plot area, use hammocks under a possible covered deck you built, convert a picnic table into a bed, throw some air mattresses outside and sleep under the stars.

The above picture shows hammocks being used outdoors but it also shows you how you can use an area such as this for dining, thus making more room within the home during mealtimes. If weather permits, there's nothing quite like being outdoors. It's healthier and a good way to enjoy the outdoors.

Chapter 13: Quotes For A New Home Build

The range of prices for which you can build a Tiny Home is as varied as the homes themselves. It all depends on what you are looking for in your Tiny Home. If you're working on a limited budget, then it is possible to build a Tiny Home for less than $10,000. If you are looking for a cheap and trendy style with everything new, then building your Tiny Home could run you $35,000 plus. The first thing to do is to decide on your budget because that will determine what your Tiny Home will cost and what materials you will look to use. We'll give you examples of both so you can see the difference.

A Tiny Home Built for Less than $10,000

141

The average cost to build a Tiny Home is $25,000, so you know it took some work and time to make this one for under $10,000. This Tiny Home is 24 feet long, 8 feet wide, and 13 feet tall. The following are some of its features.

Composting toilet, tub and shower together, and bathroom sink

Refrigerator—not full size

Double sinks in kitchen

Dishwasher

Gas range—full size

Pantry—large

Two lofts—one fits a king-size bed and the other a twin size bed

Solid stairs—no ladder

Living area with 7-foot sofa

Lots of windows and storage

Vinyl siding on exterior

Tongue and groove hardwood flooring

To build on the cheap without it looking like you did, plan on spending more time to look for bargains and then a place to store the things you find. When you find a deal, you need to purchase and pick it up right then. Waiting only gives another person the chance to grab the material before you or make a higher bid. The following tips will help you build a beautiful Tiny Home for a fraction of the cost.

Tip #1: Do All the Work Yourself

Okay, you might not be able to do all the work, but stretch yourself to do as much as you can. If you don't know anything about electricity and plumbing, you might need to seek professional help with that, but you would be amazed at what you can accomplish when you must. But when doing this ensure you're not using the time that you would normally make more money doing something your good at.

Essentially what I am saying is that if you work as an accountant or even a carpenter and you want to do the paining in your tiny home, don't take time off work to do this. Because think about it this way, if you are to make $400 a day at your normal job and you take 5 days off to paint your tiny home then you will be losing $2000 and if the tiny home could be painted in 3 days by a professional painter for $1500 then you will be losing 2 days of your time and $500. We want to be thinking and working smarter not harder!

Tip #2: Use Second-Hand Materials

Don't be surprised if you become the Craigslist king or queen as you build your Tiny Home. Look in the "for free" section on Craigslist first. Many people over-buy materials for home improvement projects, and they give the extra away if the buyer will just come and pick it up. You can find sinks, flooring, appliances, and a barrage of other things at no cost. With the popularity of renovation projects, it's a fertile field for finding used things that are still in great shape. The beauty of looking in the free section on Craigslist is that the products aren't always used, just left over from a large job. Leftovers from a larger build can be just enough to build your Tiny Home.

You can also become a frequent visitor at second-hand stores like Goodwill and Habitat for Humanity. Just because they don't have what you're looking for on the first visit, don't give up. They get different materials, furniture, and appliances in the store every day, so make these second-hand stores your favorites. The following is a list of what the owner of the above home got at Habitat for Humanity for a fraction of the cost.

Windows (from $10 to $25)

Exterior paint (five gallons for $20)

Bathroom vanity ($8)

Bathroom sink ($2.50)

Ceiling fan ($20)

Ceiling covering ($72)

Roofing foam—insulated ($70)

There are also contractor stores where you can find new appliances, sinks, tubs, and timber that might have a small blemish and cannot be installed as new in a home. They sell these items quite inexpensively, but like everything else, you must be prepared to purchase on the spot. Some of the larger stores like Home Depot and Lowe's also have a section of culled timber where you can find framing timber for much less.

You can also look for flatbed trailers on Craigslist. This homeowner found a 14-foot trailer for only $800. Make sure you check it over carefully for any rust, corrosion, or damaged metal that could create an imbalance in the flooring of your Tiny Home. Another tip—find your windows first, then build your home to fit the windows you found. Windows are incredibly expensive, and you don't have to stick to any permits or codes, so you have the potential to design your room to fit the windows you find.

Trade and Barter

Don't be shy about asking someone to trade or barter. Perhaps you have something they could use and vice versa. Or, if you have a talent or skill that is popular, ask people if they are willing to make a trade. Let them know you're working on a tight budget to build a Tiny Home. Lots of people right now find Tiny Homes quite fascinating and will be more than willing to help.

Most of all, take pride in your accomplishment of building a Tiny Home for less than $10,000. Don't point out the flaws; instead, emphasize all the ways you saved money and still created something beautiful. You rock!

Building Your Tiny Home for $40,000 Plus

One of the following Tiny Homes will probably cost you $40,000 or more. You can see that instead of vinyl siding, they have used beautiful wood, and there's a deck around the Tiny Home. They have luxury items like oversized windows and French doors, as well as skylights. All these special features add to the cost of your Tiny Home. For many, these Tiny Homes would be a step-up home from their first build. Let's review what you could expect some of the costs to be on these types of Tiny Homes.

Estimated Costs for New Items and Materials

Trailer ($5,000)

Building plans ($1,000)

Wood burning stove ($4,500)

Skylights and windows ($4,000)

Sheathing and lumber ($3,000)

Siding ($3,000)

Water heater ($1,200)

Refrigerator ($900)

Compost toilet ($1,500)

Solar system ($3,000)

Insulation ($1,500)

Flooring ($500)

Sinks, fixtures, tub, and shower ($2,000)

Roofing ($1,000)

Lighting ($700)

Propane ($1,200)

Countertops ($500)

Front door ($500)

Plumbing ($1,000)

These are all estimated prices, you can spend much more, and there are extra features and items to add to this price. These are just some of the initial expenses. If you don't plan on doing most of the work yourself, then you should also add construction costs to these figures. There's a broad range of costs for professionals, but a good rule of thumb is about $100 an hour.

Although you have your Tiny Home built, we haven't talked about where you're going to place it. Are you going to be mobile and leave it on wheels? Are you going to purchase or lease land and pour a slab on which to place your Tiny Home? There are many variables, so it's difficult to determine what these costs would be. Are you going "off the grid" or do you plan to be hooked up to city services?

Hopefully, you have addressed these questions before beginning to build your Tiny Home. Whatever your plans are, building a Tiny Home should be challenging and fun. It should stretch you and make you proud of your accomplishments. Although building a Tiny Home will test you, it's a wonderful way to build more than a home—you'll also be building self-esteem and confidence. The best thing to do as you build is to create a plan and a budget and stick to it. Refuse to let others tell you it's impossible. If others can do it, so can you.

When you are facing some of the challenges in your build, just remember this is the first step to your new life. You are building a new future with your new Tiny Home, and there are bound to be some bumps along the way. With each hurdle you cross, you'll grow and create Tiny Home experiences and memories. So, as you struggle through some of the hardships of the build, keep your eyes on the prize and know that it will soon be worth it. You and your Tiny Home have a whole new life ahead of you, and you're accepting the challenge—the first of which is in the building.

It always helps to hear from others who have gone through what you are going through and come out the other side better for the experience. Take heart! You'll be hearing some of those success stories in the next chapter.

Chapter 14: Should You Hire Someone To Build It For You?

A tiny house, like any other residential structure, needs to be constructed in the most precise manner. There is no room for mistakes when building a tiny house. Any structural weakness could cause a collapse and injure anyone near or inside the tiny house. A tiny house is also subjected to stress when moving it from one place or another. If you cut corners during construction, it will definitely weaken the house's structural integrity.

And that's a complete waste of money.

If you are not confident in your carpentry skills then hire someone to build the tiny house for you. This would ultimately mean that you'll be adding the cost of labour to your build budget but then again there is no price to put on your and other people's safety.

You could also opt to have someone assist you build your tiny house to cut down on the labour costs. That would mean you'd have to lend a hand and do some hard work. The savings you get when you choose this route is minimal but the experience you gain from working on the tiny house is priceless.

The more work you put in to your tiny house, the more knowledge you'll gain. Having intimate knowledge about the inner workings of your tiny house will prove very helpful should you need to perform any repairs in the future.

Here's another great thing about the tiny house community: tiny house owners are always willing to pitch in and help someone build a tiny house. Try to become a part of the local tiny house community in your area so you can find people willing to help you out with your project. Not only will you gain new friends through this method but you'll also be able to avoid the mistakes that often accompany first time builders with their tiny houses.

Attend lectures and seminars or workshops that involve the tiny house living to get tips and tricks for building a tiny house. This is also a great way to network and find the most cost efficient builders out there or materials available in the market.

Chapter 15: Financial Aspect: Will I Be Able To Get A Loan For A Tiny House? What About Insurance?

Cost

The cost involved in building a tiny house varies greatly from almost nothing if you can have all things donated and salvaged to $40,000 or more. In general, a tiny house will cost you anywhere between $20,000 to $25,000 in materials.

You will read a lot of things on the blogs on internet about people getting everything constructed and ready for a very meager amount. But not all such stories are true or hold any ground. If you are really think about living year on year, it will involve some money.

You should keep your ideas and parameters simple. You should ideally look at living in a home that is comfortable but does not involve you to pay loan principle and interest for the rest of your living life. You can save a lot of money by looking for reused or refurbished parts, but that involves a lot of time and effort to look for those parts which is not easy to do. Building your tiny house will involve a lot of time anyways so you could save precious time by buying the new materials instead of looking for used ones. This is especially important if moving to a tiny house is a necessity for you and time is of the essence.

Loans

If your tiny house will be on a foundation and meets all the building codes, it should not be very hard for you to get a construction loan or mortgage. Some banks, however, won't give a loan unless the house meets a particular size requirement or a certain price. Generally, these are at least 600 square feet of space and at least $50,000 in price.

If your tiny house is on wheels and if you are buying it from certified RV builder, it is possible to get a RV loan. Terms of such loans are generally shorter and interest rates higher than for normal loans. If traditional construction, mortgage or RV loans are not available for you, you can also consider private peer-to-peer lenders like **Lending Club**, **Prosper** or **Tiny House Lending**. Unsecured bank loans are also an option for those who have sufficient income. The Lightstream division of Suntrust Bank offers such loans for people who earn well.

Insurance

Insurance can be obtained easily for tiny houses built by certified and reputed RV manufacturers. If you are building your own tiny house though, finding insurance can be challenging. Before you start building your tiny house, it is advisable to contact potential companies. They may want to inspect your tiny house or see pictures of it being built.

In western USA, Lloyds of London provides limited insurance for residents of states like Arizona, California, Colorado, Nevada, Oregon and Utah. They are also trying to consider expanding to other states.

In Florida, Blackadar Insurance Agency is providing insurance for tiny houses on wheels or foundations even those that are owner-built.

Shelter Insurance has also expressed an interest to insure tiny homes in central states like Arkansas, Colorado, Illinois, Indiana, Iowa, and Kansas.

Chapter 16: Minimalism – Less Is More

The idea that simplicity can bring about happiness is an ancient one. Simple living is endorsed by all of the major religions. Buddhists rely on a simple life to keep them focused on the present moment. Followers of Islam are encouraged to abstain from luxuries and in the Christian tradition there is an emphasis on deriving meaning and satisfaction from those things which you come into the world with. It is believed that the material world separates people from their faith.

The Amish adhere to a life of simplicity – steering clear of distractions, material things and technology, all of which they feel distract them from God and from their families.

Through dress and speech the Quakers have a history of setting themselves apart from mainstream culture through simplicity. They view material excess as a burden and believe that conformity results in killing the spirit.

In modern history, we need look no further than Mahatma Gandhi - the great leader who espoused non-violence in leading India to independence allowed his ideas about living simple to infuse his way of life. It is a well-known fact that he died with fewer than ten possessions. He lived a minimalist existence by following 5 basic principles:

1. Accumulate little

2. Eat simple food

3. Dress simply

4. Be self-sufficient and do simple work

5. Let life be your message

For an idea that has been around for so long, Minimalism is largely misunderstood. While most people think it is all about managing with less, it really has more to do with adding value to life through meaning. While most minimalists favor fewer possession, distractions, clutter and waste – Minimalism is really about having purpose and choice.

THE NEW MINIMALISM

In a consumer culture, acquiring things can often feel more like a requirement than a choice – the idea that if you have more you are more is reinforced at every turn. Against this background noise it is easy to get caught up in doing things "just because". In modern life, the clutter of too many things and too much to do keeps us stuck.

A new minimalism has emerged in response to the discontent brought about by this culture which so effectively separates us from a meaningful life, and a purpose of our own choosing. As such, a new minimalism could actually be considered a counter culture.

In and of themselves there is nothing wrong with material possessions – it is the meaning which we assign to them and the requirement that we have as many as possible that is enslaving. Within a minimalist framework, everyone gets to decide for themselves what their purpose is, and what is excess in relation to it.

The journey towards a minimalist lifestyle begins for most people at some crucial point when they have cause to ask themselves how and why they have managed to accumulate so much stuff, and when they realize how invested they are in not only maintaining it but in acquiring more. Being a good consumer often comes at the expense of health, relationships and dream fulfillment — suffering a crisis in one or more of these areas often supplies a turning point.

Financial turmoil, that which is swirling around us or mounting personal debt can stop us in our tracks and cause us to question the difference between our wants and our needs. Very often we come to realize that time is actually our most precious commodity, and that wasting it in the pursuit of things precludes the fulfillment of a dream or the success of our relationships with those we love.

For some it is an emerging concern for the environment which ignites the desire for less consumption and waste. A sustainable lifestyle certainly uses fewer of the earth's valuable resources.

Sometime a person may turn to minimalism through an appreciation of a modern aesthetic – only to realize that stripping down to the essential is calming and that this principle can be applied to other areas in life such as scheduling.

However you arrive, as an emerging minimalist you will begin to develop a desire for more time, money and freedom, but particularly more meaning in your life. You will need to figure out what is important to you and begin to manifest this in your daily life.

MOVING TOWARDS A MINIMALIST LIFESTYLE

All change in life begins with an idea. Only when it is put into action and repeated until it becomes a habit is change solidified. Moving towards a simpler lifestyle is not easy, but it is worthwhile.

If you believe that the way to happiness is not through things and you can begin to cut to what is essential– but you should also begin to question what adds value to your life. Decide for yourself what is really important and begin to construct your life around it.

Often this process will take you out of the realm of the material. In addition to possessions, we often hang on to habits (certain ways of doing things), ideas and people which weigh us down and inhibit our personal freedom. Decluttering principles can also be applied to obligations and thought patterns if these keep us from focusing on what we know to be important. Don't forget the goal of the minimalist is more time, money and freedom, but also more meaning.

BENEFITS OF MINIMALISM

1. More Money: Financial freedom may result from spending less and not working more.

2. More Time: You'll spend less time shopping, cleaning, and maintaining possessions.

3. More Focus: When your environment is less cluttered so is your mind.

4. A Change in Focus: You'd be surprised how holding on to things can have the effect of keeping you focused on the past rather than grounded in the present.

4. Less Stress: Less debt and activity will go a long way towards decreasing stress. A decluttered environment is less frenetic visually, and you will have more time to focus on a healthy lifestyle – eating, sleeping and exercising well.

5. Less Waste and Excess: You will be contributing to a healthy environment.

SAMPLING THE MINIMALIST LIFESTYLE

Human change is precarious at best, and you will have better luck if you ease into minimalism, rather than going whole hog. Here are some guidelines to help you get started slowly.

1. Examine your current lifestyle, and try to identify your reasons for wanting to live more simply (I hate my job, I have no time with my kids, I can't sleep at night are all great reasons).

2. As exhaustively as possible, list everything in your life: things, activities, people, but also persistent ideas and habits. Rate how vital each of this is to your life.

3. Ask yourself how you managed to acquire all of this stuff in the first place.

4. Ask yourself what you were missing out on while you were focusing on accumulating all this stuff.

5. Start by getting rid of anything you have doubles of – this is painless and liberating.

6. Try to stay focused on the ways in which you will be adding value to your life with less in it.

7. Start to question your purchases when you go shopping. Ask yourself if you really require what you're buying, or if you're filling some other need.

8. Seasonal items aside – get rid of anything you haven't seen or used in the last 5 months.

9. Organize what you do have.

10. Think about living with fewer clothes.

11. Think about living in a smaller place.

12. Eat less variety – try rotating 3 or 4 basic meals.

13. Turn the TV off for a week.

14. Keep the kitchen countertop clear for a week.

15. Remove excess furniture from rooms for a week.

16. If you own a garage, think about this as a place to park the car rather than as a storage facility.

Chapter 17: Reasons For Not Living In A Tiny House

I know that I've stated this multiple times, but it's important to note that the tiny house lifestyle isn't for everyone. Not everyone will find it appealing. Not everyone will like it and it will be a big mistake if you built the entire house just to find out that you don't want to live in it. Ask yourself this: Are you actually passionate constructing and/or residing in a tiny house? Will living in a tiny house negatively affect your lifestyle in some way? Here are some other reasons why you "shouldn't" live in a tiny house:

You have kids accustomed to their own space

You have important family members or friends who frequently visit you, and they do not like the tiny house lifestyle

Your significant other does not like the idea

You have a lot of pets. Pets need the freedom to roam.

You enjoy collecting objects (or hoarding for the matter). The tiny house itself will not have enough space to store all of your collections

You have many objects that you depend on. I personally know someone cannot live without his Desktop, 70" smart screen television, and Xbox. Those are large items. Perhaps, the tiny house lifestyle isn't for him.

You're claustrophobic. Perhaps I don't need to tell you that since living in a tiny house will never cross the minds of a claustrophobic person.

You're a shopaholic. Again, the tiny house life style is for minimalists. You won't be able to find the space to store all of your items

You or a family member has a physical disability. As a disabled person, you may not be able to deal with loft/climbing ladders. You need more space around you to cope.

There are also three primary complaints by people who are against tiny houses. I will let you decide whether or not these statements are true:

Tiny houses are not sustainable - The main argument against living in a tiny home is that it's not sustainable. Consider some of the following questions: Will your family grow to include additional family members? Do you or your family members prefer privacy? What are you going to do when you're too old to climb over your kitchen to get in your bed? Where are you going to store personal keepsakes that you don't want to part with?

Living in a tiny house is too expensive – Forbes reported that the average cost of creating a tiny house is $200 to $400 per square foot. Yes, the overall cost is cheaper, but the ratio of cost to size is much higher for a well-designed tiny house than for a regular American home. The 2010 Census breaks down the average cost of a new, single family house at just over $85 per square foot. That is considerably lower. A quick check reveals that the cost of a tiny house is around 2-5 time higher than the average cost of a single family house.

Potential legal issues – Zoning in a random location can pose a legal issue. Since many tiny houses are on wheels, they can run into issues with municipalities that have little to no legal establishments for tiny house residents. This doesn't mean that living in a tiny house is illegal, but rather that many regions of the country aren't set up to allow for an easy transition to a tiny house lifestyle. For instance, safety precautions are often ignored and hooking up utilities can be potentially difficult. This can lead to expensive and time-consuming legal challenges.

If you are able to address some of these concerns and are still interested in the tiny house lifestyle, good for you! Perhaps the tiny house living might still make sense for you. The main point is to be mindful. Benefits can include lower utility bills (or not utility bills), less of a temptation to fill your house with expensive items, and no mortgage at all.

The desire to live a more frugal life and be free of the debt heavy life are great things to pursue. Just be sure to consider all costs, including long-term ones, before you decide to move into a tiny house. Ultimately, the best frugal choice for you depends on what works best for you, rather than just the size of your house.

Conclusion

It is evident from this book that construction of your tiny house on a strict budget is not as challenging as we initially thought possible. This is because of the proper steps employed during the building process as well as proper budgeting of the money that we have available for the entire project.

Many of the steps we have mentioned in this guide are suitable for beginners who wish to focus their energy on putting up a tiny house that meets their needs. The activities herein are easy to do by yourself as well as through the help of a professional hired at a cost.

You have to realize that dividing the operations of the building process into simpler steps makes the whole project of construction quite easy. This is especially the case if you already know the sequence of events that the project will follow from the beginning to the end.

The use of this guide is very helpful and beneficial when you are designing your tiny house on a budget. This helps positively impact your surrounding positively by taking up less power and limited space.

www.ingramcontent.com/pod-product-compliance
Ingram Content Group UK Ltd.
Pitfield, Milton Keynes, MK11 3LW, UK
UKHW021733170225
4629UKWH00042B/619

9 781990 268991